For the ones I love, Cathy, Claire, Maddy and Tom – L.A.

JANETTA OTTER-BARRY BOOKS

First published in Great Britain in 2012 by Frances Lincoln Children's Books, 4 Torriano Mews, Torriano Avenue, London NW5 2RZ
www.franceslincoln.com

A catalogue record for this book is available from the British Library.

ISBN 978-1-84507-911-6

Illustrated with watercolours
Set in Zenke Hand and Bembo

Printed in Dongguan, Guangdong, China by South China Printing in January 2012

1 3 5 7 9 8 6 4 2

visit the Anholt website: www.anholt.co.uk

PHOTOGRAPHIC ACKNOWLEDGMENTS

Page 8 below left: *Portrait of Joseph Roulin*, (1889) by Vincent van Gogh.
Museum of Modern Art (MOMA), New York (Gift of Mr and Mrs William A.M Burden, Mr and Mrs Paul Rosenberg, Nelson A. Rockefeller, Mr and Mrs Armand Bartos, Sidney and Harriet Janis, Mr and Mrs Werner E. Josten, and Loula D. Lasker Bequest (by exchange). 196.1989. © 2011. Digital image, The Museum of Modern Art, New York/Scala, Florence

Page 13: *Self-portrait with a Straw Hat*, (probably 1887) by Vincent van Gogh.
(Verso: The Potato Peeler). Metropolitan Museum of Art, New York. Bequest of Miss Adelaide Milton de Groot, 1967 (Acc.n: 67.187.70a) © 2011. Image copyright The Metropolitan Museum of Art/Art Resource/Scala, Florence

Page 14 below left: *Bull's Head*, (1942) by Pablo Picasso.
Musée Picasso, Paris. © Succession Picasso/DACS, London 2011. White Images/Scala, Florence

Page 14 below right: *Baboon and Young*, (Vallauris, 1951) by Pablo Picasso.
Museum of Modern Art (MOMA), New York. Mrs Simon Guggenheim Fund. 196.1956. © 2011.
© Succession Picasso/DACS, London 2011. Digital image, The Museum of Modern Art, New York/Scala, Florence

Page 19: *Woman with Baby Carriage*, (1950) by Pablo Picasso.
Hirshhorn Museum and Sculpture Garden, Smithsonian Institution. Gift of Joseph H. Hirshhorn, 1972.
© Succession Picasso/DACS, London 2011. Photography by Lee Stalsworth

Page 23: *Studies of Flying Machine*, (Ms. B 2037 f. 80r.) by Leonardo da Vinci.
Institut de France (Bibliothèque), Paris. © 2011. Digital image, Scala, Florence

Page 29: *Little Dancer of Fourteen Years*, (1881) by Edgar Degas.
Musée d'Orsay, Paris. © 2011. White Images/Scala, Florence

Page 33: *The Codomas*, plate XI from 'Jazz', (1943-47) by Henri Matisse.
Museum of Modern Art (MOMA), New York. The Louis E. Stern Collection. Acc. num. 930.1964.11.
© Succession H. Matisse/DACS 2011. Digital image, The Museum of Modern Art, New York/Scala, Florence

Page 39: *The Rose Path at Giverny*, (1920-22) by Claude Monet.
Musée Marmottan, Paris. Photo: akg-images

Page 43: *Green Apples*, (1873) by Paul Cézanne.
Musée d'Orsay, Paris. © 2011. White Images/Scala, Florence

Anholt's Artists
ACTIVITY BOOK

LAURENCE ANHOLT

F
FRANCES LINCOLN
CHILDREN'S BOOKS

Contents

The activities set out in this book are a lot of fun but you must ask an adult before using sharp or dangerous materials. Activities are carried out at your own risk. The author and publishers disclaim all responsibility for accidents which may occur.

Introduction

Paint a Portrait with Vincent van Gogh

You will need: large sheets of paper or card fixed to a board; a set of water-based paints (like poster paints or acrylics); a paper plate for a palette; brushes and jars of water; an easel if you have one; and lots of courage.

Vincent is famous for his swirly brush marks and bright colours. Some of my favourite paintings are the portraits Vincent made of people he knew... like this picture of my father....

Don't be scared! It's not as hard as you think... Let's get set up.

A bright background will make things more exciting, so I'm pinning this lovely sunflower fabric on the wall.

Now you need to ask someone to be a model. It could be a relative or a friend. They will have to sit very still.
Will you sit for me, Vincent?
Of course I will, Camille!

Pin a big sheet of paper or card on to your board and squeeze out some colours on a plate or palette. It's good to stand up if you can – painting should never be fiddly!
If you shine a light on one side of your model's head, it creates a more dramatic effect.

Vincent's Tip – 'JIGSAW SHAPES'

Here's something really important about painting which many people never think about – the spaces around the figure are as important as the figure itself. These are called 'negative' shapes. Look at any great painting and you will see that the negative and positive shapes all fit together to make a composition. The shapes lock together inside the picture frame like pieces of a jigsaw. Lots of people paint a figure floating around in a great white space. But here's the trick – the stronger you make the negative shapes, the more powerful your picture will be.

NEGATIVE SHAPES

POSITIVE SHAPES

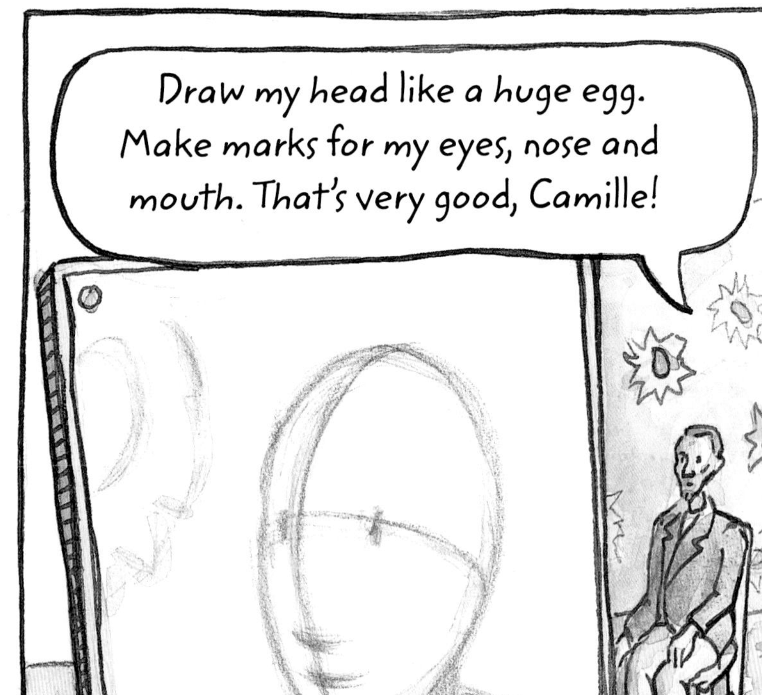

VINCENT'S SECRET:

Be careful not to put the eyes too high on the head.

In fact eyes are about halfway between the chin and the top of the head.

Now begin to paint in large areas of colour. Make the colours bright and strong.
Don't use grey or dull colours.

Look carefully, Camille. Can you see interesting or unusual colours within the shadows? For example, the side of my head which is in shadow might have cool blues or purples.
Don't be a scaredy-cat, have fun with the colours.

Save the details until later. If you start with details, it's like putting windows in a house before the walls have been built!

Even great artists don't get things right straight away. It's fine to keep changing things – that's what painting is all about. Just paint over what you have done until it begins to work.

Keep looking at the model all the time. Try squinting your eyes – can you see that one side of the head is dark and one side is light? That's what will make your painting look round and solid as an apple.

When you have covered the whole piece of paper with big bold shapes, it's time to start adding details like the lips, eyes and ears. Look at my paintings – you will see that I use a small brush and a strong colour like blue to draw outlines.

Well done, Camille. That is a wonderful painting! I always sign my pictures. Why don't you sign your own name? It takes a lot of practice to paint like an artist. The main thing is to be BRAVE and have FUN!
Camille

Thank you for the lesson, Vincent. You are the bravest painter of all. I have learnt so much from you.

Chat About Art

Vincent was a lonely man. People laughed at his paintings. They couldn't see that the strange man with the yellow beard was one of the greatest artists who ever lived. Read *Camille and the Sunflowers* and chat about tolerance and prejudice and the way in which some people are 'outsiders'...

Self-portrait with a Straw Hat

In what ways are people different? How would you relate to someone who was different from you? Would you be kind to them like Camille or would you be a bully? Perhaps that person has hidden abilities, which we do not notice because they look different, or have a different background or way of talking.

Search for portraits by these great artists:

VAN GOGH, GAUGUIN, REMBRANDT, LUCIAN FREUD FRIDA KAHLO, ERNST KIRCHNER.

Make a Funky Junk Sculpture with Picasso

You will need: a collection of disused objects and materials; string or wire; strong glue; a basic tool kit if available; and lots of imagination.

A bull's head made from a bicycle seat and handlebars

A baboon made with two toy cars for a face

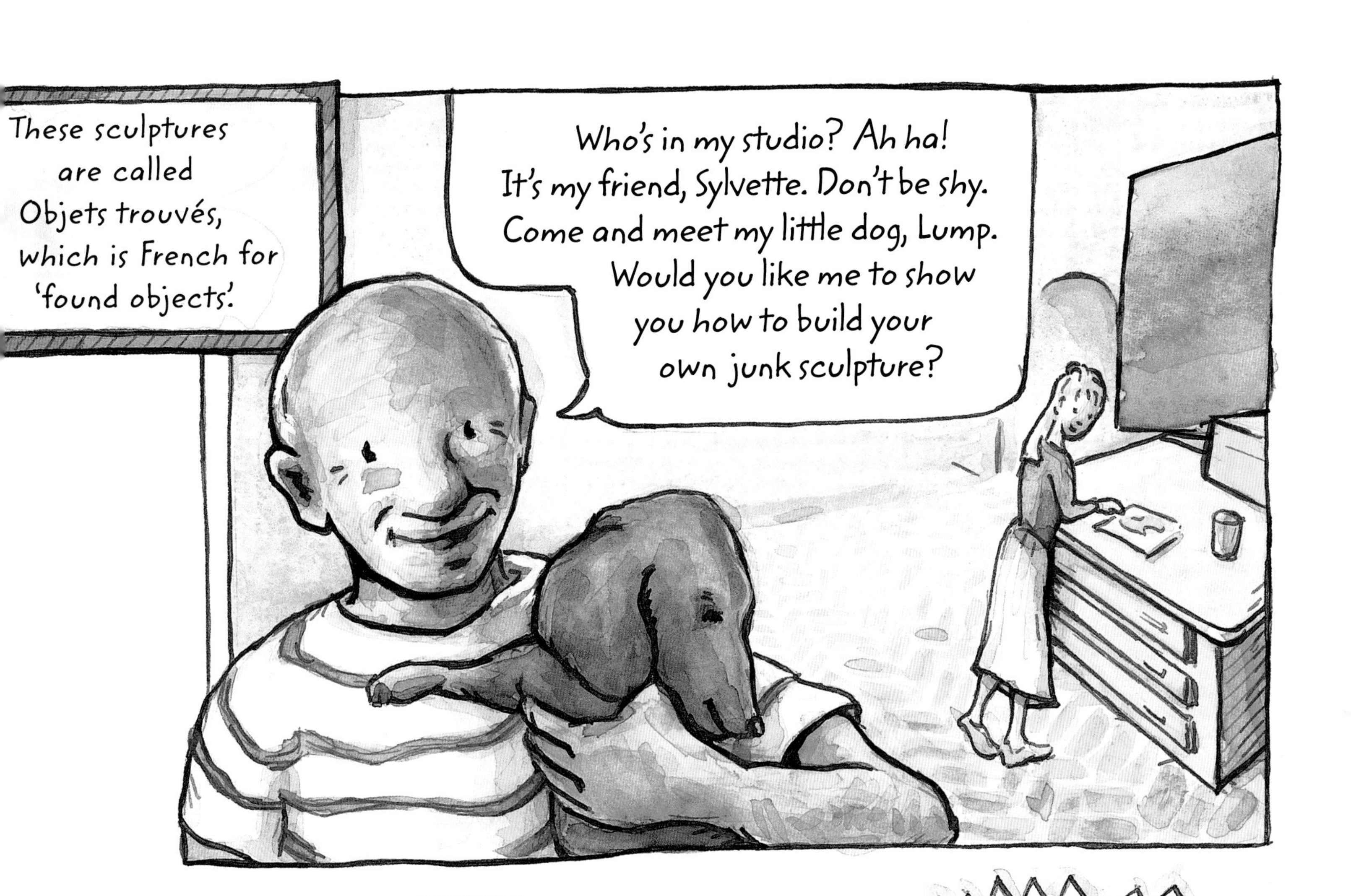

WARNING

NEVER TOUCH ANYTHING SHARP OR DANGEROUS. AVOID BROKEN GLASS AND DO NOT OPEN JARS OR BOTTLES IF YOU DON'T KNOW WHAT'S INSIDE. IF IN DOUBT, ASK AN ADULT.

You can find interesting junk in your garage, attic or kitchen, or go to a car boot sale – broken toys are great and the beach is a wonderful place to find stuff.
What have you found, Sylvette?

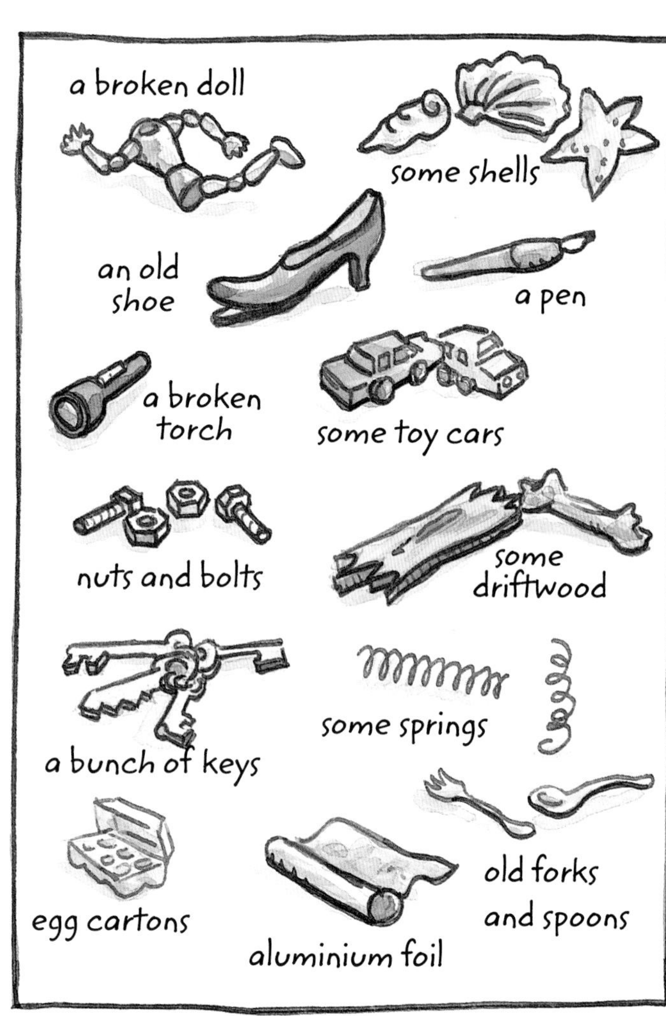
a broken doll
some shells
an old shoe
a pen
a broken torch
some toy cars
nuts and bolts
some driftwood
a bunch of keys
some springs
egg cartons
aluminium foil
old forks and spoons

What magnificent junk! We'll also need some wire and glue. I've got my tool kit. Now, start by holding different objects together. Look for interesting combinations.

I've made the dog's head with an old shoe. If I make a body with a card-board tube, it looks a bit like Lump!
socks for ears
spring
spoons

That's very good, Sylvette.
We can join things together with wire, string or glue. Ask an adult to help with screws or nails. There are no rules – you can use plaster and fabric too.
If it doesn't work straight away, you can pull bits off and change them.

SECRET:
Let it all change. Whether you are painting, making sculptures or even writing stories, it's very important to let things change and grow while you work. Pull bits off, stick new bits on – and don't worry.

You can also make a hanging sculpture called a mobile…

or make a 3d junk painting by sticking objects on to a board.
I'm pouring sand into the wet glue.

Sylvette has made a tiny sculpture...
bird skull
toy soldier

but I prefer to work BIG like my sculpture of a mother and baby."

If you want, you can paint your sculpture in crazy colours.

That's the thing about being an artist – you are in charge, you make the decisions.

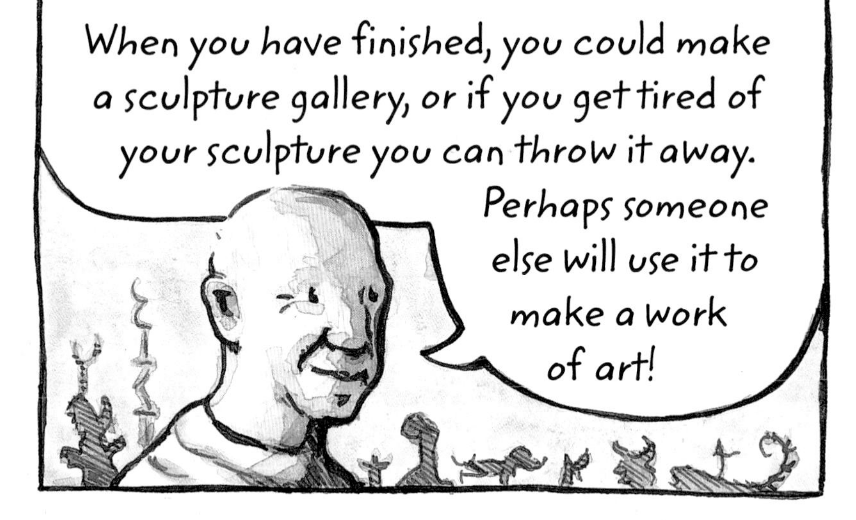
When you have finished, you could make a sculpture gallery, or if you get tired of your sculpture you can throw it away. Perhaps someone else will use it to make a work of art!

Thanks for the idea, Picasso. You have shown me how to make a masterpiece from garbage!

Chat About Art

Pablo Picasso started making art when he was a small boy. He became one of the most famous and richest artists who ever lived and he was never scared of inventing new ways of making art. In his life, he created more than 30,000 amazing paintings, sculptures, drawings, and prints.

In 1954, Picasso met Sylvette David, 'the girl with a ponytail'. Sylvette was a very shy girl, but Picasso helped her to become an artist herself and now she works every day in her own studio.

Picasso was a genius, but do you think a genius is born that way or can anyone become a genius? Read *Picasso and the Girl with a Ponytail* and talk about genius. Does it help if people praise what you do? Have a look at the last secret in in this book: being confident.

Woman with Baby Carriage

Search for sculptures by these great artists:
PICASSO, RODIN, ANTHONY GORMLEY,
BARBARA HEPWORTH, GIACOMETTI, HENRY MOORE.

Leonardo's Mad Marvellous Machines

You will need: large sheets of paper; brown paint (or some very strong tea!); pens or drawing materials; lots of crazy ideas.

SECRET:

I don't mind Zoro peeping in my notebooks. He won't be able to read my ideas because I use a

TOP SECRET CODE.

Look, I have used 'mirror writing' – I write back to front...

so you can only read
my writing in a mirror.

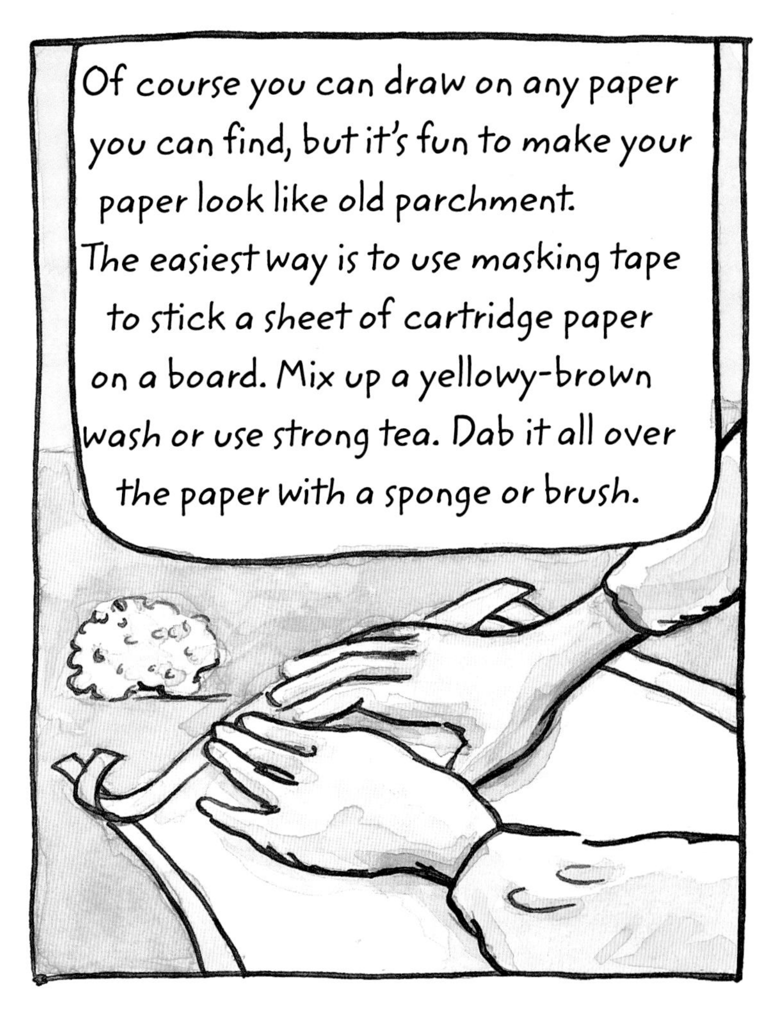

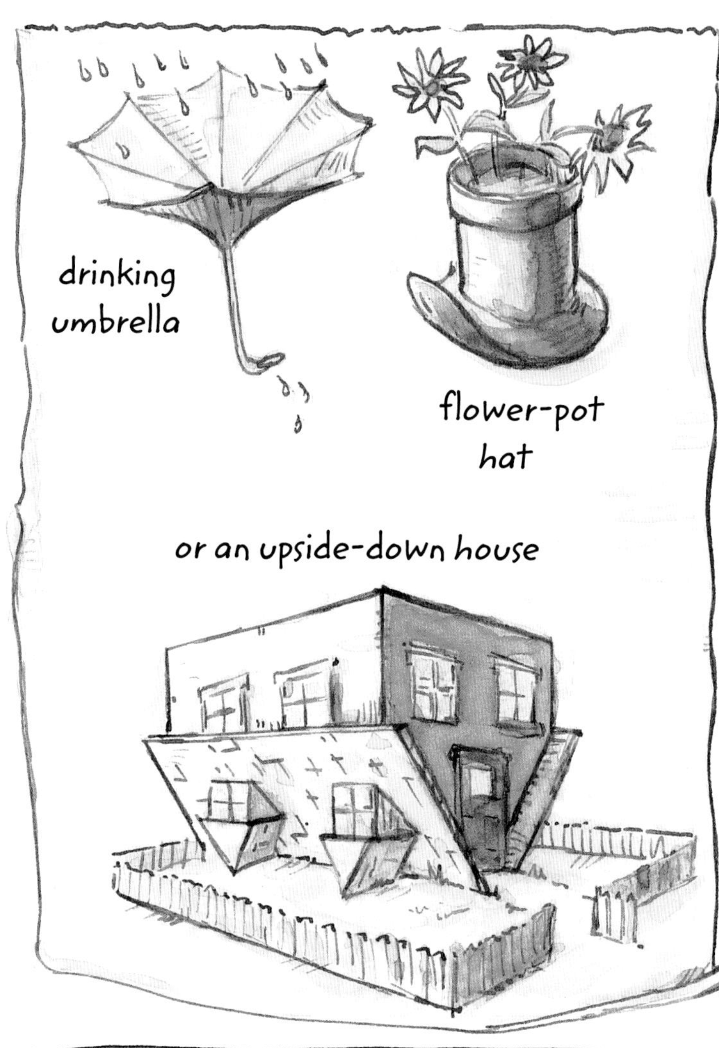

Just let your imagination go! Now it's time to sketch out your invention on our parchment. Start in pencil so you can rub out and make changes. When you are ready, draw over the pencil line with a pen. If you use brown ink it will look just like an original Leonardo! Let's see what Zoro has invented.... My goodness! A flying bicycle! Come back, Zoro!

Chat About Art

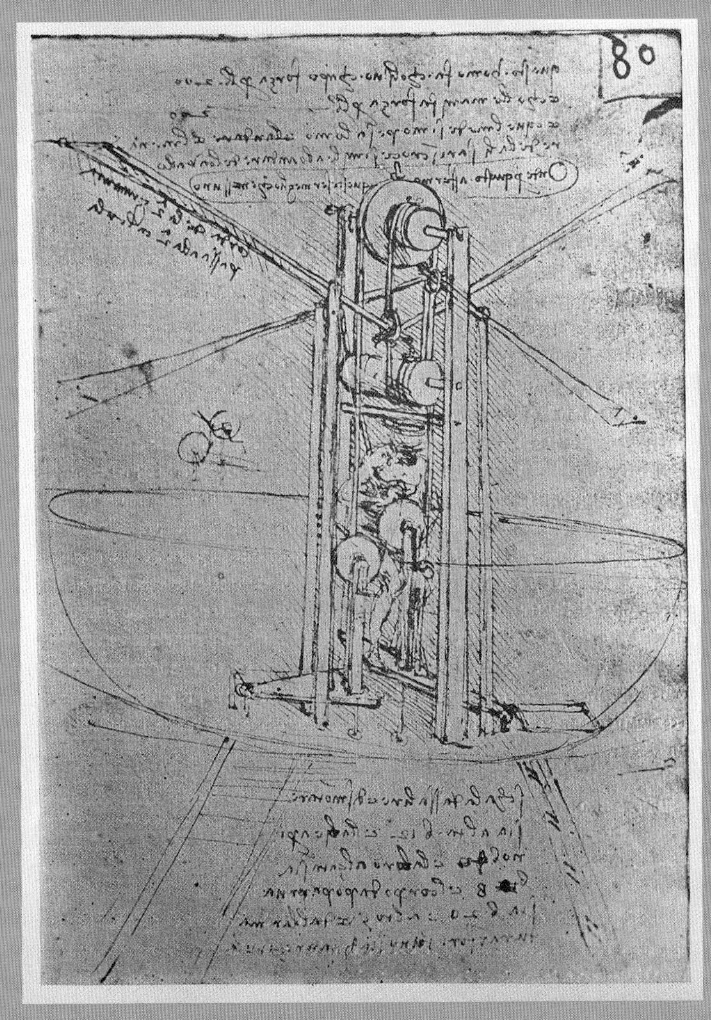

Studies of Flying Machine

Leonardo da Vinci was born in 1452 (almost 500 years before Picasso). This great genius had the amazing idea of making a drawing of every object in the world – of course he didn't succeed but perhaps the internet has come a bit closer to making his dream come true. Leonardo lived during the Italian Renaissance. Renaissance means 'born again' and this was a time of many wonderful inventions and great art.

Are we living in a Renaissance now?

Perhaps this is a Technological Renaissance (computers and robots) or a Green Renaissance (ecology and alternative energy)?

What do you think people will say about our world in 500 years time?

Search for amazing inventions by these artists:
LEONARDO DA VINCI, W. HEATH ROBINSON,
RENÉ MAGRITTE, M.C. ESCHER, JEAN TINGUELY

Art in Action with Degas

You will need: some self-drying modelling material – there are many types available, eg 'Das,' 'Plasticine' and 'Sculptamould'; alternatively make Papier Maché with shredded newspaper soaked in diluted PVA adhesive; you will also need wire such as coat-hanger wire or sculptors' aluminium armature; rubber gloves; and lots of patience.

but here are some pictures of wrestlers.
And here are some dancers.

Very good, Marie. Now I suggest you take a good look at your photos and make a few sketches.

SECRET: Drawing Figures
Here are some tips for drawing people...

1
Look for an 'Underlying Rhythm,' in other words some kind of movement which runs through the whole body. Sketch that in lightly.

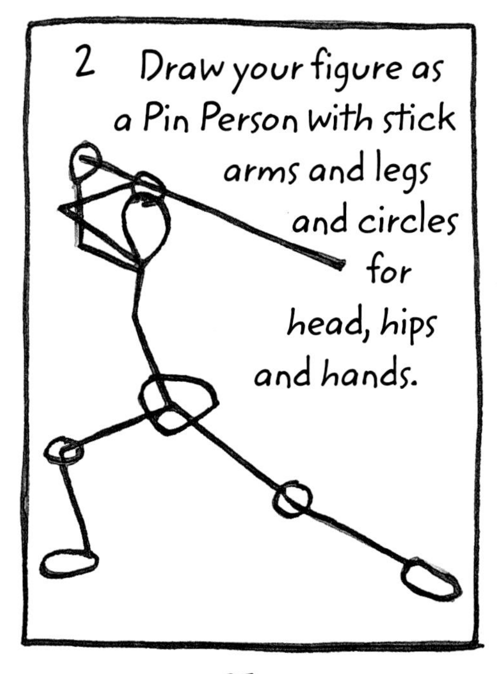
2
Draw your figure as a Pin Person with stick arms and legs and circles for head, hips and hands.

3
Finally add muscle, hair and clothes.

Look, Monsieur Degas, I have made a study of a skateboarder!
Monsieur Degas! What are you doing...?

I like to try out the position myself. It helps me to get the feel of the pose.... Why are you laughing, Marie?
Hee, hee! I'm sorry, Monsieur Degas.
Now pay attention before I get grumpy.

That's good, Marie. We're nearly ready to start. But there's one more important stage – we need to make an armature. An armature is like a skeleton inside the sculpture.

SECRET:

In 2002, a team of scientists at the National Gallery in London took an x-ray of my sculpture of the Little Dancer. They discovered my secret – I made armatures out of wire, pieces of wood, tin lids, bottle tops and even old paint brushes! I was making it up as I went along.

You can make an armature with sticks or bendy wire. Have a good look at your reference photo and make a Pin Person like the one in your drawing.

NAILED TO BASE

I often make my sculptures in wax and I even stick on real fabric or hair, but there are all kinds of materials you can use to make sculptures – the easiest is Plasticine but it might get squashed. My favourite material is papier maché and it's almost completely free! Papier Maché is easy to make....

Humph! I must admit this bit is quite good fun! We are wrapping the papier maché (or modelling clay) around the armature. Slowly build up the thickness of the arms and legs.
It's easy to pull bits off too and stick more on.
When you are really happy, let your model dry nice and slowly.
Finally you can paint your model, and if you want to work like me, you can add scraps of real fabric or any materials you please.

Thank you so much, Monsieur Degas. It's been a hard day but I am very pleased with my action sculpture.
It was fun working with Degas and he was hardly grumpy at all.

MAGNIFICENT, Marie!

Chat About Art

Little Dancer of Fourteen Years

Degas was passionate about ballet. He made hundreds of images of dancers. Do you have a passion for something? It might be dancing, sport, writing, singing or travel. Read *Degas and the Little Dancer* and discuss how you could use your passion to inspire your art. Is it better when people have a job which is something to do with their passion?

Search for Movement in Art
by these great artists:
DEGAS, UMBERTO BOCCIONI,
JACKSON POLLOCK,
GEORGE BELLOWS,
BRIDGET RILEY, BALLA.

ONE LAST THING

When you draw or make a model of a figure, you can tell if the proportions are correct by using the FRANKENSTEIN TEST! Imagine your drawing or sculpture coming to life and walking around the room. Would the proportions look right or have you created Frankenstein's Monster with a huge head or tiny legs? Aaargh! Run for it!

Matisse's Cool Colour Creations

You will need: lots of sheets of thick paper – sugar paper is fine; a set of bright water-based paints such as Acrylics or Poster Paints; a large decorator's brush; good quality scissors; glue sticks or PVA adhesive; some music to inspire you!

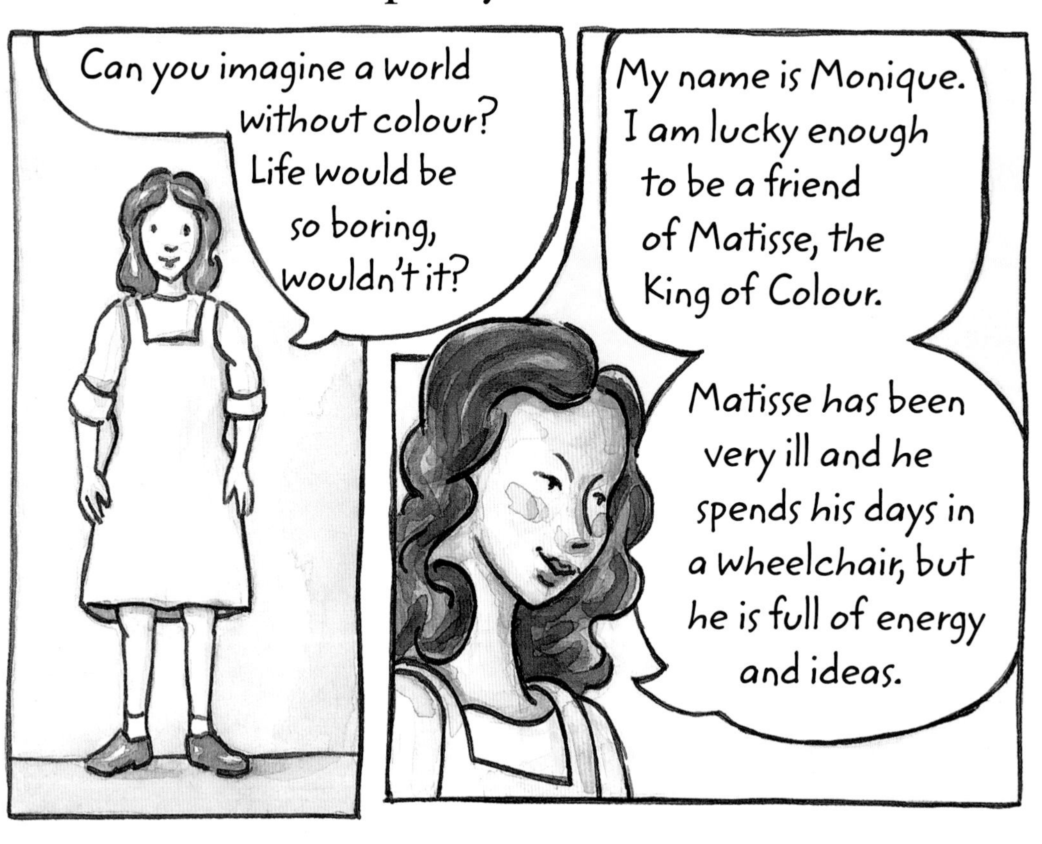

Put some music on and let's get started. Work outside or put down lots of newspaper – this is going to be messy.

First, paint lots of sheets of paper with bright colours. Cover the whole surface and make them as BRIGHT as possible. It's fine if you can see the brush marks. Now we have to wait for the paint to dry.

OK, now take your scissors (ask an adult first), get into a nice relaxed mood and just begin to DRAW WITH SCISSORS!
I'm making a whole pile of wonderful, colourful shapes – some spiky, some smooth; some thin, some fat; some wiggly, some starry!

If you run out of ideas, just look at the shapes all around you – the shapes of leaves, bowls, hands, faces, animals or patterns of fabric.

When you are happy with your pile of colourful shapes, take one large, coloured sheet of paper and begin to arrange your shapes – big shapes first and small shapes after; but don't stick them yet.

SECRET:
a good composition will work upside-down or back-to-front! Look at any great painting upside-down or in a mirror and you will see that the composition is just as strong. Get into the habit of doing the same thing with your own work.

Now I am carefully sticking my shapes in place. I marked the position with a pencil so I know exactly where they go. I loved making cool compositions with Matisse!

Chat About Art

Disability – many artists had some kind of mental or physical impairment: Degas and Monet suffered from visual impairment, Matisse spent the last part of his life in a wheelchair and Van Gogh had serious mental problems. Read *Matisse, King of Colour*, and talk about the way in which disabilities affected some great artists' work. Perhaps their work would not have been so exciting if they were 'able-bodied.'

The Codomas, plate X1 from 'Jazz'

Search for cool colours by these artists:
MATISSE, DERAIN, KANDINSKY, BONNARD.

ONE LAST WORD

If you want to try something really interesting, you can make pictures which describe a feeling – for example red spiky shapes may look ANGRY. Smooth blue shapes may appear CALM. What happens if you only use dark colours – or just light colours? Have fun finding out.

Monet's Wild Wet Watercolours

You will need: some sheets of thick paper – cartridge paper or proper watercolour paper is best; a set of watercolour paints and brushes; jars of water; a soft cloth or kitchen paper; and a lovely view!

Try half-closing your eyes until everything blends together.
It all looks blurry!

We are going to work with watercolours in a special way… it's called 'WET INTO WET'.

You see, Julie, the beautiful thing about watercolour is the way one colour runs into another. Sometimes the best effects happen by chance.

Let's practise on some spare paper.

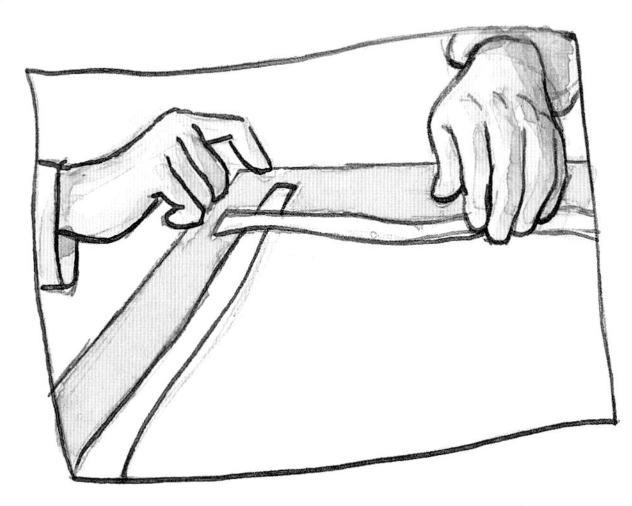

1 First fix your paper on to a board.

2 Then make the paper slightly damp all over.

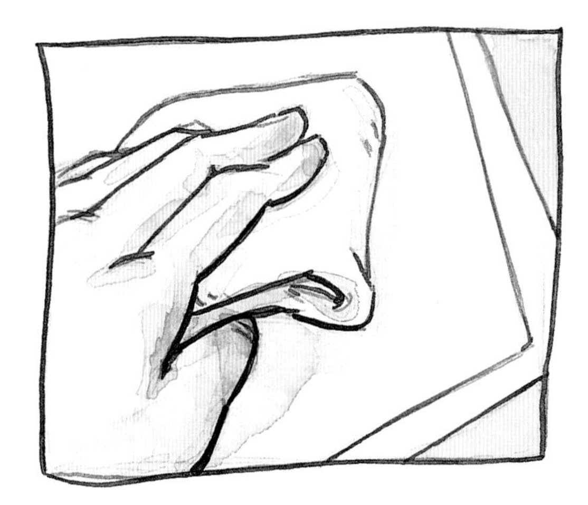

3 Use kitchen paper or a rag to dry off any excess water.

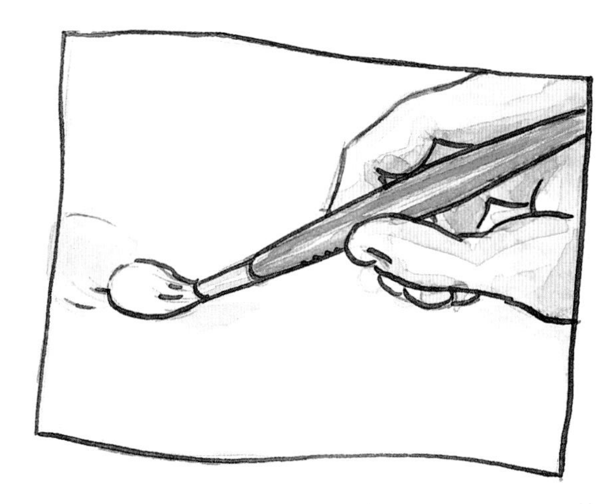

4 Now paint a strip of very wet yellow. This is called a wash of colour.

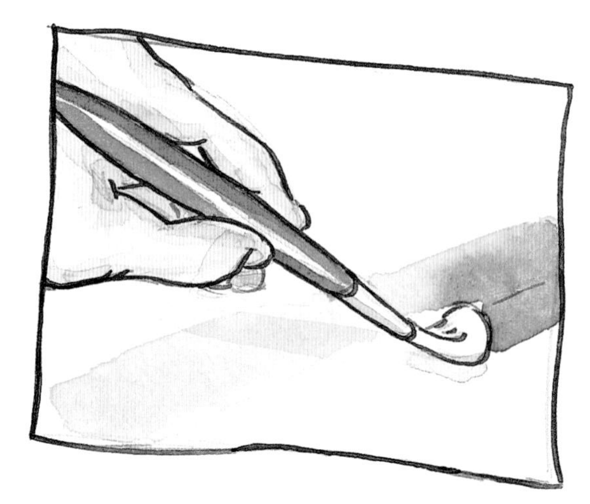

5 Next to it paint a strip of very wet red.

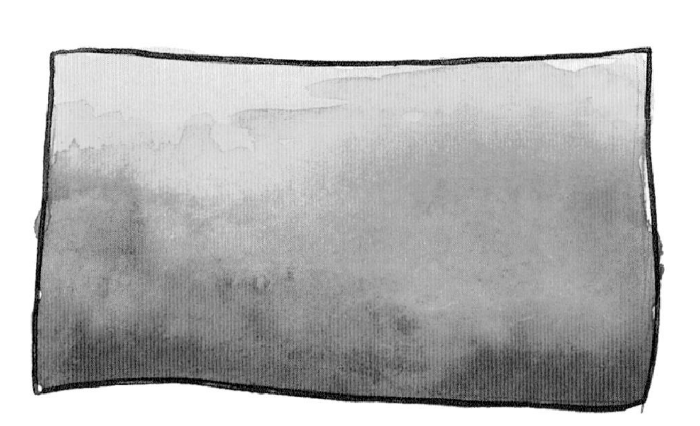

6 Let the two colours touch and you will see they blend to make a beautiful orange.

It's fun, isn't it?
Look, I'm trying the same thing with other colours – yellow and blue make green. Blue and red make violet....

TIP: Keep your colours clean. Have one jar of water for washing brushes and another jar of clean water to mix with your paints.

Good. Now we're ready to make a painting.
Take a good look at your view – that's right, Julie, squint your eyes....
Let's paint the bridge over the waterlily pond.

Make your paper slightly damp all over and start to paint very freely. Begin with the sky or the background, and keep your colours very pale to begin with – so mix in lots of clean water.

You may feel a little out of control, but don't panic! With watercolours, there is nothing better than a HAPPY ACCIDENT!

After a while, the paper begins to dry a little, so now you can add some details in the foreground which will be sharper and darker.
When your painting is really dry, you can even draw into it with pencils, crayons or pen and ink.

That was a beautiful painting, Julie.
Thank you, Mr Monet. You taught me to go with the flow.

Chat About Art

The Rose Path at Giverny

As he got older, Monet's eyesight became very poor and everything seemed blurry. But it didn't stop him from painting. Some of the last pictures he made are blurry too but they are full of colour and atmosphere and many people think they were the best paintings he did. Do you think paintings need to be 'realistic' like photographs or are you more interested in 'abstract' qualities like atmosphere or expression?

ONE LAST THING: Seeing like an alien

If you see the same street or the same view every day, you may think it isn't very interesting. But the things which artists paint are just ordinary too – van Gogh painted old chairs and a pair of boots; Monet painted trees and skies – they just learned to see the beauty in ordinary things. So here's a great trick... imagine you have landed on this planet from outer space. You are seeing things for the first time! Every street is strange; every tree is extraordinary; and what about those weird things called people? When you see like this, you realise that our 'ordinary' world is amazing. If you look at it in this way, even a crumpled piece of paper is as astonishing as mountains covered in snow! You are looking at the world with an artist's eye!

Read *The Magical Garden of Claude Monet*,

and search for atmospheric paintings by these great artists:

MONET, TURNER, CASPAR DAVID FRIEDRICH, EDVARD MUNCH.

Also look at the lovely art by Julie's mother, Berthe Morisot.

Cézanne's Charcoal Challenge

You will need: some sheets of strong paper – sugar paper is fine; some sticks of charcoal which you can buy at any art store; an old rag or kitchen paper; a hard, plastic rubber; some hair spray!

I have to warn you that some people get a shock when they see my father. You see, he is very tall and he looks a little wild, but don't be scared – he's really very kind and he has promised to show us how to draw with charcoal.

TIP: CHARCOAL IS GOOD FOR ROUGH, TOUGH DRAWING, SO DON'T GET FIDDLY!

First, just rub some charcoal across the paper to get rid of that horrid white.

Rub it in with your rag or with your fingers.

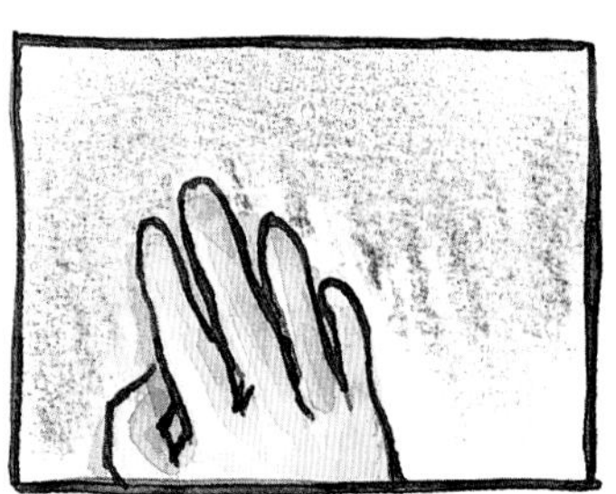

Now sketch in bold, simple shapes. If you make a mistake just rub it with your rag.

With charcoal, you get a whole range of tones. Use shading to make your shadows.

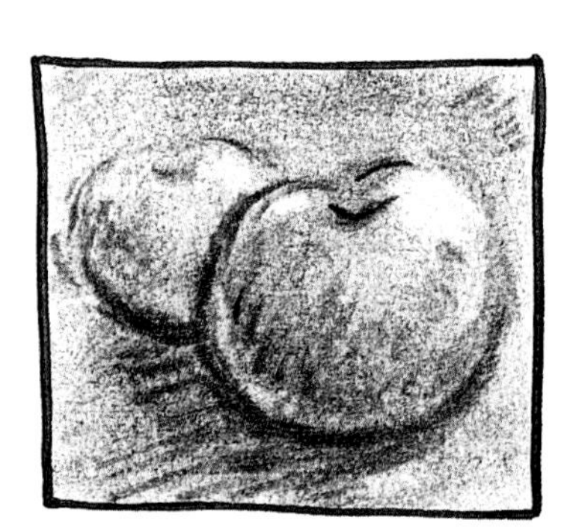

If you want, you can lightly blend the tones with a finger or a rag.

Use the tip of a rubber to put in highlights. Now your drawing begins to look real.

Chat About Art

Green Apples

Cézanne was inspired by nature. He spent much of his life walking and painting in the wild mountains of Provence. If the weather was poor he would often paint apples or portraits in the studio.

Read *Cézanne and the Apple Boy* and discuss the importance of nature in your own life – what is the wildest place you have ever visited? Have you ever been completely alone in nature? How did you feel?

Search for images of Nature by these great artists:
CÉZANNE, TURNER, GEORGIA O'KEEFFE, ANDY GOLDSWORTHY, CONSTABLE, FREDERICK CHURCH.

If you are serious about being an artist, you should set up your own Art Cupboard where you can keep all your materials. Or you could have an Art Bag like my rucksack. I carry it wherever I go and it's full of paints, sketch books, brushes, charcoal, rags and everything I need to create a work of art.

LAURENCE ANHOLT'S SECRET

I hope you enjoyed making your own masterpieces.
I have one final tip and it's really the most important one of all... BE CONFIDENT!

Imagine you are starting a drawing. Suddenly a friend comes over and starts to boss you around and laugh at your work – "What are you doing?" they say. "Your drawing is terrible! I have a baby brother who is a better artist than you!"
Well, you wouldn't be very happy, would you? In fact you probably wouldn't feel like drawing at all after that.

In my experience, most of us have a bossy voice inside our heads... do you? When you start a new project, do you hear a doubtful, negative voice telling you that you're no good? It's perfectly normal. The trouble is, if you want to be an artist (or anything else, for that matter) you need to be CONFIDENT! You need to trust your instincts. You can't even concentrate when your bossy friend is there.

So here's what to do...Tell the bossy voice (very politely) to go away.
Tell them you are busy... please can they come back later. THEN... change the bossy voice for the voice of your VERY BEST FRIEND...
"WOW! You are doing a painting! What fantastic colours! I think you must be the best artist I know!" Imagine what that would be like! You wouldn't worry at all if your best friend was there.

So that's all there is to it – talk to yourself in a kind way. Don't criticise yourself. Be your own best friend. And remember what Leonardo said.

"Anything is possible!"

ANHOLT'S ARTISTS

Collect all Laurence Anholt's brilliant books
about artists and the real children
who knew them.

Camille and the Sunflowers

Cézanne and the Apple Boy

Degas and the Little Dancer

Leonardo and the Flying Boy

Matisse King of Colour

The Magical Garden of Claude Monet

Picasso and the Girl with a Ponytail

Don't expect your artwork
to look like any of the pictures
in this book. It will be something
new! That's because you are
an ARTIST too.

ARTIST